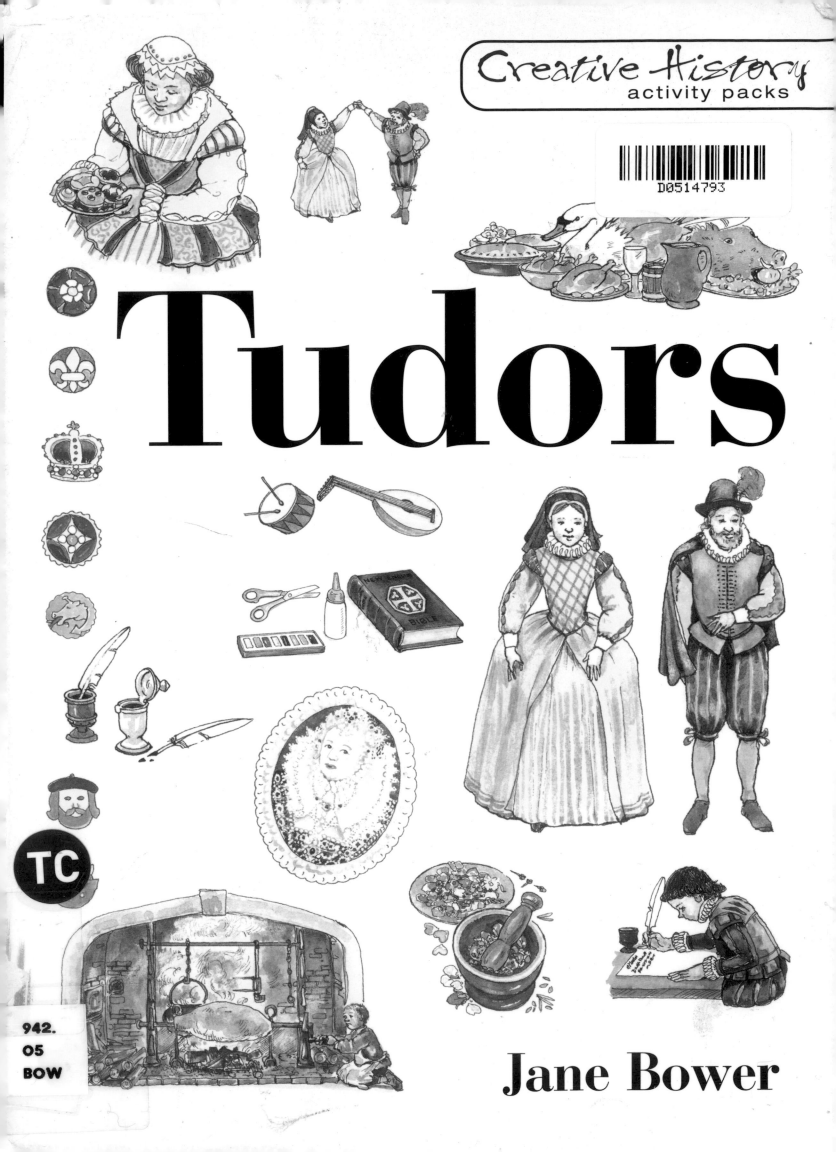

Creative History
activity packs

# Tudors

## Jane Bower

# Tudors Pack

## *Learning Objectives*

This pack addresses key areas of both the study unit Life in Tudor Times (NC KS2 history) and NC KS2 art, as well as aspects of drama, dance, and design and technology. Through using the activity cards, children are given practical opportunities to:

- learn about aspects of court life
- explore ways of life in town and country
- understand more about home life, work and leisure, health and trade
- develop an appreciation of the art and crafts of the period and recognise how these reflect the time in which they were created
- compare ideas and methods of the past with those of today
- find out about the art, music and clothing of the time
- design and make images and artefacts
- explore a range of materials, tools and techniques
- record from observation, instructions, and their own knowledge and imagination
- respond imaginatively to historical facts through role play
- interpret music of the time through dance
- build a presentation or performance and present it to an audience
- plan, design, modify and develop the starting points given, to make further artefacts with similar characteristics.

## How to use these cards

These cards have been designed by experienced primary teachers who have carried out many of the activities with one or more classes, or large or small groups, on many occasions. The cards have been written chiefly for use by teachers or other adults in charge of pupils, but we have worded them so that they could also be used directly by a capable child or small group, at the teachers' discretion. The cards are deliberately not numbered – they are designed to be used in a completely flexible way to complement, extend or introduce aspects of a topic on Tudors. Teachers can use some or all of the cards, in any order which is appropriate to their work.

**Jane Bower** trained at St Martin's College of Education in Lancaster, and has a degree in Art and Design. She was a full-time primary teacher in Lancaster and the Lake District for twelve years. She is now a part-time primary teacher and an independent consultant/adviser in KS1 and KS2 art, drama and dance, travelling to primary schools countrywide. She also works as a teacher for History Off The Page. Jane writes regularly on practical classroom arts activities for several educational journals including *Child Education* and *Five to Seven*, and produces teachers' workpacks for BBC Schools Radio Drama.

**History Off The Page** comprises a team of experienced primary teachers who travel individually to British schools in England and Europe. They offer a wide range of stimulating, authentic hands-on history days, using original materials, artefacts and role play for up to 90 children, covering all the NC periods including Tudors, Greeks, Romans, Egyptians, Victorians and Vikings for KS2; and special KS1 days including Castles and Toys.

For further details on support from the ...ff The Page or Science Off The Page, please phone/fax 01954 21...281, ema... ...demon. ...o.uk or write to History Off The Page, The Old School, Har...dwick, Cambri...

Meanwhile, in the Hampton Court kitchens below, it is a different story. The servants have been preparing the vast meal of many courses for the last few days. There are no fridges, so everything has to be done quickly. The servants could lose their jobs if the king or queen is not pleased.

Again, everyone needs to choose a role.

Servants worked in:

the flesh larder (meat)
the wet larder (fish)
the spicery
the chaundry (candles)
the boiling house
the bakery

Gallopynes were young boys who had the dangerous job of turning the spit.

See cards 'Write a Tudor Menu', 'Sweetmeats and Subtleties' and 'Butter and Biscottes' for ideas on what foods you might be preparing. The huge kitchen is hot from the roaring fire and the cook is under severe stress!

A suitably bustling piece of music can be used to accompany the activities. This, when contrasted with the graceful dance of the upstairs guests, can be worked into a short presentation (perhaps with added narration), or can form the content of a drama lesson.

# Upstairs, downstairs

Explore contrasting sides of Tudor life through drama.

Drama helps us to understand the feelings of other people by imagining we are those people. Begin by looking at photographs of Hampton Court or similar*. Notice the fine, richly decorated rooms. Imagine that a vast banquet is to be held here, and decide on the reason for this. For example: one of Henry VIII's marriages; the birth of Prince Edward; the coronation of Henry or Elizabeth.

Everyone in the class then chooses a role as a guest at the banquet. One could play the monarch, and others might include:

Master of the Revels, Lord Steward, Master of the Horse, Ladies in Waiting, Privy Councillors, Chaplain, Nobles, Musicians, Courtiers.

Find out or discuss what these people did.

Special clothing has been ordered from London for the occasion. In role as the guests, open the chests containing the clothes in the privacy of your own candlelit, panelled bedchamber and put them on. (See list of clothes on 'A Tudor Dance' card in this pack.) Descend the grand staircase, and after conversation with the other guests (probably about the reason for the banquet), bow as the king and/or queen enters and perform your stately dance.

* Historic Royal Palaces Information Line – 020 8781 9500

Next, decorate circles A and B using the paints and black pen. On one side would be a decorative design such as a Tudor rose or a circular pattern. On the other side would be a verse or line from the Bible. Try looking in the books of Psalms or Proverbs for suitable quotations.

Glue the reverse of the flaps only on circle A and bind them over the card circle. Stick circle B on the other side to cover flaps.

If you are going to use the posy plates to serve sweets (see 'Marchpane Sotleties' card) you may like to cut two 11cm circles of sticky-backed plastic to cover and protect the two sides.

Posy plates were specially made for the occasion of a visit by Elizabeth I to William Cecil.

# Posy plates

At the end of a meal in rich Tudor houses, sweet cakes or marchpane sotleties were served on posy plates (also known as roundels).

To make one posy plate you will need:

stiff card cut in a circle (about 11cm diameter) • scissors • glue • a sheet of white A4 paper • paints • a fine paintbrush • black pen • Bible • clear sticky-backed plastic (optional)

Use a compass cutter to cut the circle from the stiff card, turning it several times until the circle falls out cleanly. Place the card circle on the A4 paper and draw round it twice, allowing a 2cm margin around one of the circles, as shown.

Cut around the unbroken lines. Snip into circle to make flaps as shown.

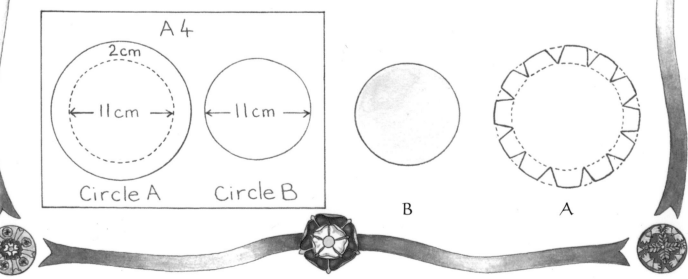

Try the scene to some lively Tudor music.

For the second part of the drama, ask the children to move back into groups of three or four.

Traders in Tudor times belonged to a Guild, and meetings were held in the Guild Hall to discuss rules and air grievances. Visit each group to help them decide on a grievance to bring to the meeting. These might include:

- the state of the roads (perhaps your horse had an accident, or you lost your load and arrived late)

- the number and danger of cutpurses (perhaps you lost all your day's takings)

- the lack of hygiene (there are open sewers, and flies around your meat; customers have complained of illness after eating it)

- someone is not trading fairly (you have evidence that his/her scales are faulty – purposely or otherwise?)

You (the teacher) can take the role of convener of the Guild meeting. Each group can air their grievance and this can be thrown open for general discussion, always remaining in role as Tudors. Can other traders support or refute the evidence given? A vote can be taken as to whether the trader accused of cheating is guilty or innocent. If he/she is found guilty, the drama can end with a ducking in the village pond!

N02382

# A Tudor market

The lives of Tudor traders explored through drama

To the teacher:

Before beginning this drama you may like to find some books, information or pictures about Tudor shops and market places to show your class. Introduce the drama by explaining that you are all going to experience two aspects of Tudor trading through role play. Ask the children to get into groups of three or four and discuss the following:

Who are you, or what do you trade? (e.g. a farmer's wife selling butter, eggs and cheese; a butcher in the Shambles (benches for cutting meat); a customer wanting fruit, a tooth pulled or a cure for warts)

What is your sign? (a symbol such as a barber's pole was needed for customers who could not read)

How do you and/or your goods get to market? (e.g. a horse-drawn wagon; a boat across the river – Tudor roads were often full of large holes; on foot with a pack, etc.)

If you trade, do you have any special cries? (rhymes or phrases to advertise wares, e.g. for hazelnuts 'Brown and round, a groat a pound', or 'Apples ripe and juicy!')

## The market place

On a given signal, bring the market place to life – cries, weighing goods on the scales, selling to fussy customers, bargaining, chopping meat or fish, wrapping butter . . . One or two children could be cutpurses (pickpockets), sneaking between the crowds.

Instead of marchpane you can try SUGAR PASTE.

To make sugar paste you will need:

450g icing sugar • 4 teaspoons powdered gelatine • 2 teaspoons liquid glucose • 4 tablespoons cold water • colouring (or try cinnamon, ginger, saffron or carrot juice as the Tudors did)

Sprinkle the gelatine on to the water, and leave it to go spongy. Then dissolve it over hot water until the mixture goes clear. Add the glucose and leave until melted. Sieve the icing sugar and make a well in it. Add the liquid mixture and stir till well-mixed. Knead before modelling. Tip: a tiny touch of white lard on the fingertips keeps the paste pliable.

If you would rather keep your elaborate models than eat them, you could make them from PLAYDOUGH – it looks similar to marchpane.

To make playdough you will need:

200g plain flour • 100g salt • 2 teaspoons cream of tartar • 1 tablespoon cooking oil • 300ml water containing food colouring • large pan

Put all ingredients in the pan. Heat and stir well for a few minutes until thick and stiff. Turn out the dough, cool and knead well before modelling.

Display your models on posy plates (see 'Posy Plates' card).

N02382   Part 9

Pack

# Sweetmeats and subtleties

Sugar was an expensive and luxurious treat in Tudor times. It was fashionable to end a banquet with an array of stunning sweets modelled in sugar. These would be made by the lady of the house rather than the cook. A report of a meal in 1527 records castles, churches, beasts, birds and a chess set modelled in sugar, and even plates and goblets were made from it for guests to take home.

Because of nut allergies, three alternatives are offered here: two to eat and one to keep.

## Marchpane (marzipan) sotleties

To make marchpane sotleties you will need:

Ground almonds • twice the weight of icing sugar to almonds • rose water (OR bought marzipan) • food colouring • large bowl • boards • cocktail sticks or modelling tools

Mix the almonds (the Tudors would have had to grind these with a pestle and mortar) with the sugar and add only enough rose water to make a stiff paste. Divide paste and add a little colouring. Try modelling crowns, dragons, Tudor roses, the King's and Queen's entwined initials – the more detailed the better.

Tudor dance steps were to some degree dictated by the clothing worn (and possibly the huge meals eaten) by the dancers.

Choose a piece of Tudor music with an easily recognisable rhythmic beat which is not too fast ( e.g. CD Popular Music from the Time of Queen Elizabeth I, Saga Classics, EC 3352-2, tracks 15 and 17, or track 3 (slow), or track 5 (faster)).

## Building your dance

Dances would usually begin with a reverence – girls mime holding skirt out and curtsey, tucking one leg behind the other and bending the knees; boys mime removing hat and bow slightly from the waist, one foot in front of the other. (The stiff stomacher prevented low bowing and the starched ruff prevented bending the neck.)

Children can work in groups of 4–6 and devise a simple repeated sequence to the music using steps of the time. Their group can form a circle, square or two facing lines. Examples of steps to a beat of four could include:

- step forward, step back, 2 beats to turn round
- put right hands in to form a star, 4 steps round in circle
- 2 children make arch with arms, others step through

Groups can perform their own sequence simultaneously with other groups' interpretations, or a selection of favourite ideas can be used to form one dance for everybody. Keep steps stately, controlled, small and on the beat. Finish with another reverence.

# A Tudor dance

If you wish, this Tudor dance can be used as the culmination of or to complement a piece of drama (see 'Upstairs, Downstairs' and 'A Tudor Market').

It adds greatly to children's appreciation of Tudor dance if they first carefully mime dressing for, say, a celebratory ball. Copy the red wording* below on to a large chart, put it on the wall and cover with a blu-tacked sheet. Move the sheet down one item at a time, as each garment is 'put on'.

| Maids | | Fellows | |
|---|---|---|---|
| 1 | Chemise (vest with lots of buttons or tapes | 1 | Shirt (fastened with buttons or tapes) |
| 2 | Silk hose (stockings – no elastic, tapes to tie) | 2 | Silk or satin hose (see Maids 2) |
| 3 | Drawers (knickers with tapes round waist) | 3 | Drawers (see Maids 2) |
| 4 | Farthingale or bum roll (holds dress out from body) | 4 | Breeches (trousers ending at knee) |
| 5 | Stomacher (richly embroidered top of dress, with bone or wooden stays on front, point ending at stomach) | 5 | Stomacher (similar to Maids 5) |
| 6 | Kirtle (underskirt) | 6 | Petticoat (waistcoat: petti is from 'petit', i.e. little) |
| 7 | Sleeves (separate items tied to stomacher with 'points' or tapes) | 7 | Doublet (jacket or jerkin) |
| 8 | Gown (skirt section of dress – rich and heavy, put on over head) | 8 | Gown (cape thrown over shoulder) |
| 9 | Ruff (starched, so neck held upright | 9 | Ruff (see Maids 9) |
| 10 | Cork-heeled shoes (often high) | 10 | Square-toed shoes |
| 11 | Jewellery and paint | 11 | Plumed hat |

If clearly explained and well mimed (avoiding exaggeration), children should be able to sense the physical restriction such clothes would impose, and their understanding and dance movements will be more accurate.

* the black wording offers additional information for the teacher

Fold the three 10 x 16cm sheets centrally to form the pages. Using the bradawl on the wooden board, make three holes down the fold. Sew all three sheets together with the needle and thread.

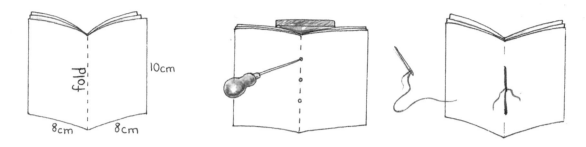

Place the brown paper covers (16 x 10cm) under the two stiff cards (9 x 12cm) as shown (see diagram (a) below). Cut off the corners (shown in red). Glue only the flaps (shown in brown), not the main part of the cover, and fold them over the card (see diagram (b) below).

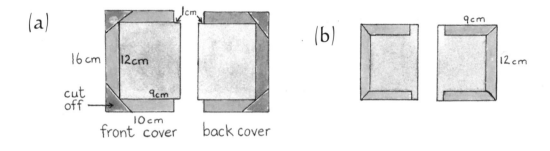

Turn the covers over, place them ½cm apart, and glue on the leather (17 x 6cm) to overlap the edges of the covers (see diagram (c) below). Turn covers over again. Fold over the ends of the spine and glue down inside the book (see diagram (d) below).

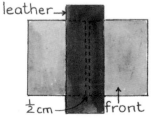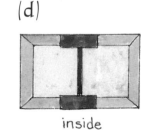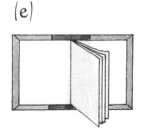

Stick the front and back pages to the inside covers of the book (see diagram (e)). Leave the book standing open until completely dry.

# A handmade book

Here is a simple hand-bound book which can be used to house Tudor recipes, pressed flowers or herbs, prescriptions or prayers. Try using hand-made ink to write in them (see 'Make Your Own Ink' card).

To make one book with ten pages you will need:

2 pieces of stiff card, 9 x 12cm* • 3 sheets of white paper 10 x 16cm • 1 piece of thick paper or thin leather 17 x 6cm • 2 pieces brown parcel paper 16 x 10cm • glue • bradawl • wooden board • needle • scissors • strong thread

To give your pages the look of parchment, you can dip a teabag in tepid water and wipe it over both sides of the three white 10 x 16 sheets. Allow to dry thoroughly.

The Tudors did not have brightly coloured paper. Keep the colours of the book muted, or use handmade paper if you have any.

*the measurements given are suggestions – the books can be made smaller or larger as necessary.

# Soapballs

The Tudors rarely immersed themselves in water, and their understanding of the importance of cleanliness was limited. But they did use soap. They made theirs from animal fat and woodash, but this stage has been omitted here!

To make soapballs you will need:

white household soap • coarse cheese grater • pinhead oatmeal scented water (e.g., orange or rose water*) saucers • pestle and mortar • sweet-smelling plants (e.g. lavender, rose petals)

Grate the soap into a saucer – one bar should make 2–4 soapballs. Add a very small amount of scented water, a drop at a time, until you are able to push the soap together. It should not be wet. Add a pinch or two of oatmeal (used to exfoliate the skin). Grind your chosen plants in the mortar to release the scents and add to the soap. Push the mixture together until you can roll it into a ball (these can vary in size from a marble to a tangerine) adding more drops of scented water if necessary. Allow to dry.

*from The Body Shop or supermarkets

# Clove pomanders
## and Soapballs

The Tudors did not have flushing toilets, and in many areas rubbish was disposed of in the streets. These pomanders could be carried when walking, to hold to the nose when the street smells became too unpleasant.

For each pomander you will need:

scissors • an orange • 60cm of ribbon, 1cm wide • 2–3 handfuls of cloves • 2 dressmaking pins

Cut 20cm of ribbon and wrap it tightly around the middle of the orange. Secure with a pin. Cut another 20cm of ribbon and tie the two ends together to form a loop. Pass the final 20cm of ribbon through the loop and wrap vertically around the orange, securing with a pin. Stick the cloves into the exposed areas of the orange, fairly close together but not touching, as the orange will shrink as it dries. The cloves help to prevent it from going bad.

In a wardrobe, a drawer, or standing in a room, your pomander will sweeten the air.

The Tudors had no standardised spelling, so there are various versions of the word 'biscuit' in recipe books, including 'bisket', and 'biscotte', which came in many forms. Gilded gingerbread, bisket bread, cracknels, jumbals and Naples bisket were all popular sweetmeats to end a banquet, and could be dipped into flavoured butters.

To make JUMBALS you will need:

2 tablespoons melted butter • 125g sugar • 125g flour
60g ground rice • 2 egg whites • 1 egg yolk • $1\frac{1}{2}$ teaspoons rose water

Whip the sugar and egg whites together until creamy. (To be authentic, you should do this by hand. One Tudor recipe calls for a biscuit mixture to be beaten for two hours . . .)

Add egg yolk, flour, melted butter, ground rice and rose water.

Grease and flour a baking sheet. Drop teaspoonsful of the mixture on to it, allowing room for the jumbals to spread.

Bake at 400°F/ 200°C, gas 5, for 8 minutes.

Cool on a wire rack and serve with the decorated butters flavoured with sugar or rose water.

# Butter
# and biscottes

To the Tudors, butter was not an accompaniment to serve with bread as it is today, but was a dish in its own right. It was offered as an alternative to cheese, or flavoured with sweet or savoury additions. It was decorated in various elaborate ways before being brought to the table.

To make dishes of butter you will need:

double cream • a glass jar with a screw-top lid • wooden bowls or boards • modelling tools and/or butter moulds • flavouring such as garlic, herbs, rose water, sugar • fresh herbs, e.g. parsley

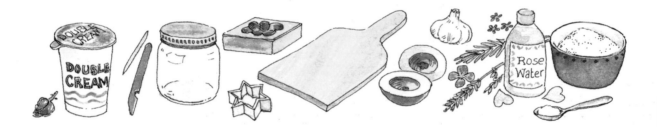

Ensure that the jar, lid, bowls, boards, moulds and tools are sterilised by pouring boiling water into or over them, emptying them and leaving to air dry. Place the empty jar and cream in the fridge until cold.

Pour the cream to half-fill the jar and take turns to shake it vigorously until a lump of butter forms. Drain any liquid out, then add flavouring, beating it well in. Shape the butter into flowers or patterns. Decorate savoury butters with carefully placed herbs. Serve on boards or in wooden bowls.

Mark the head lightly in pencil and paint the flesh tone. Paint in the features and hair over this. Then paint in the background – this was usually blue.

To be really authentic, you can paint your miniatures on old playing cards, as the Tudors did. You will need water-based acrylic paints, which will cover the designs on the cards.

The Tudors used shells to mix their paints in. Use a blob of blu-tack to stand shells in to keep them steady.

Finally, make a frame for your miniature by gluing on gold beads or tiny pasta shapes painted gold. To wear it as a necklace, hang from a gold thread, or attach a safety pin to make a brooch.

Useful reference: the artist Nicholas Hilliard, 1547–1619.

# Miniatures

The Tudors had no photographs, so the only way they could record someone's face was by asking an artist to paint it. Miniatures were tiny portraits small enough to carry or wear as jewellery.

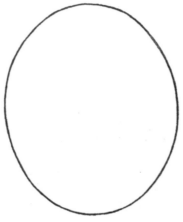

To make a miniature you will need:

white card • paints • small brushes • water • glue • tiny pasta (e.g. farfalline pasta bows) and gold paint OR small gold beads

Decide who the subject of the miniature should be. It was often someone whom the owner loved and wanted to keep in mind. Mark out an oval about 5 x 4cm — you can trace the one above as a template. This is the actual size of a Tudor miniature in the Victoria and Albert Museum in London.

# Write a Tudor menu

The Tudors' diet was not well balanced. They ate a huge amount of meat and bread, but few vegetables. A banquet could have many courses and last for several hours.

To make a menu you will need:

Tudor ink and quill (see overleaf) • white A4 paper • teabags • a bowl of tepid water • books to research your menu • scrap paper • pencils

Ducke, fowle and pidgeon well stufft
Rosted swanne in ye sauce of plummes
Wild boare with apples
A sallet of herbes
A pye of spyced myncemete
Sweetmetes and sotleties
Ale and Meade

Dip a teabag in the water and use it to paint the white paper to give the look of parchment. Allow to dry thoroughly while you plan your menu on scrap paper. Write out the menu for a banquet, perhaps for Henry VIII, using your Tudor ink and quill (and perhaps Tudor spelling!).

# Make your own ink and Tudor menu

Ink has been made in various ways throughout history. Here is one of the methods the Tudors used.

To make ink you will need:

oak galls ('oak apples' found on oak trees – not acorns!) • iron sulphate tablets or powder* (from garden centres or chemists) • water • pestle and mortar • wooden skewer or quill • scrap paper •

Crack, crush and grind an oak gall in the mortar. This can take some doing, but the more finely you grind it, the better your ink will be. Add one iron sulphate tablet or half a teaspoonful of powder. (The Tudors would have obtained this from rocks.) Add just enough water to make a liquid ink. Try using a quill pen – a goose feather with the end cut on a slant with a craft knife, to make a point as shown.

* Care should be taken when using these ingredients